C. 1   3/88   B&T 8/6.94

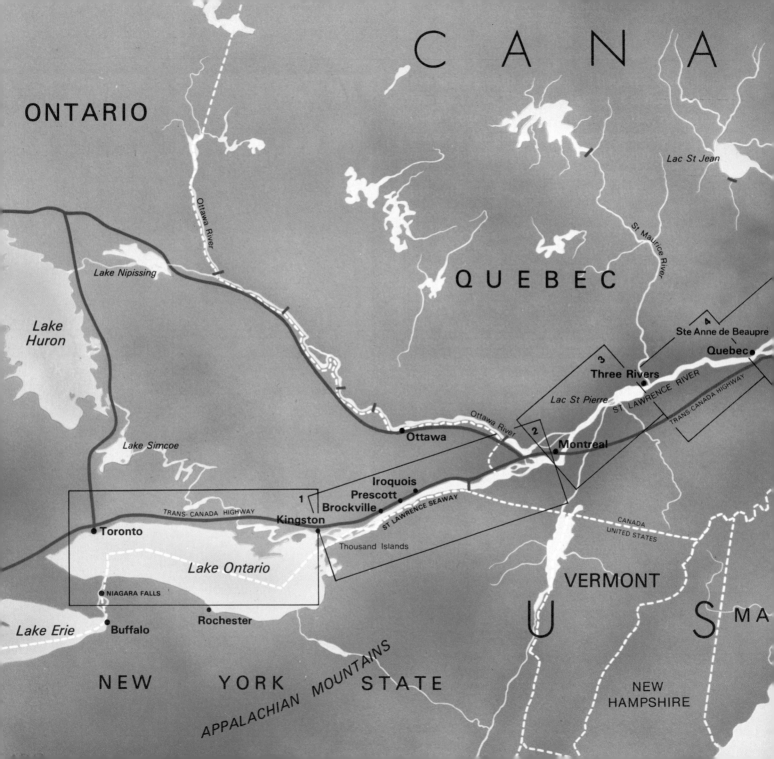

Authors
Robin W. Winks is Professor of History at Yale
University. He has travelled widely throughout the world,
and is the author of a number of books on Canada and the
United States. Honor Leigh Winks, his daughter, is an
art historian.

Series Consultant
Dr E. B. Worthington is a consultant ecologist with a
particular interest in hydrology. He was President of the
Committee on Water Research of the International
Council of Scientific Unions.

The St Lawrence

The St Lawrence river has always been used as a great
routeway. For its first European explorers, searching for a
passage to China, it was the entrance to the vast, and then
unknown, land of Canada. Along its banks settlers built
their farmsteads, founded Canada's greatest cities, and
fought the Indians. Making their way far inland along the
river, they set up the fur trade — exporting the furs back
along the St Lawrence and across the Atlantic to Europe.

The modern St Lawrence has been altered and controlled
to make an even greater trade route. Its rapids have been
bypassed, its changing levels overcome by the use of locks,
and its force has been harnessed to produce electricity.
Since the completion of the St Lawrence Seaway, the river
forms part of a huge waterway stretching from the
Atlantic to the head of the Great Lakes. Appropriately,
the French explorer Jacques Cartier, who discovered the
St Lawrence, called it 'the River of Canada'.

The St Lawrence

Honor Leigh Winks &
Robin W. Winks

Wayland/Silver Burdett

Rivers of the World

Amazon
Colorado
Congo
Danube
Ganges
Mississippi
Nile
Rhine
St Lawrence
Thames
Volga
Yellow River

© Copyright 1980 Wayland Publishers Limited
First published in 1980 by
Wayland Publishers Limited
49 Lansdowne Place, Hove
East Sussex BN3 1HF, England
ISBN 0 85340 734 7

Published in the United States by
Silver Burdett Company
Morristown, New Jersey
1980 printing
ISBN 0 382 06368 6

Printed in Italy by G. Canale & C. S.p.A., Turin

Contents

Introduction: the River of Canada

The St Lawrence has been called 'the River of Canada' — an appropriate name, for it has played an important part in the history of that country. When Europeans first discovered Canada, it was through the Gulf of St Lawrence that they entered the country. Settlements developed and trading sites grew up along its banks. Today, harnessed by man's engineering skills, the St Lawrence provides Canada with hydro-electric power and a waterway that is vital to commerce.

The St Lawrence was not always the great waterway that it is today. Millions of years ago, before any water flowed between its banks, a soft bed of rock ran along an ancient formation of hard rock known as the Canadian Shield. Volcanoes erupted and earthquakes changed the balance of the land, causing soft rock and hard rock to press together until the soft rock slowly sank, allowing the sea to come in and cover it.

During the Ice Age, a great mass of ice pressed the soft rock further into the earth. Thousands of years later, this sunken portion of the earth moved back upwards. Before the region could return to its original state, however, the sea flooded it, forming a vast body of water. The bed still continued to rise, causing the area of water to shrink. Another depression was also rising. Thus what is now known as the Great Lakes area was once a single body of water. As the land rose, the fresh water spilt out and rushed through inland valleys to the sea.

So the St Lawrence was born. Where the softest rock once was, the river widens out. At three places it is so wide that lakes have been created in the river. On our trip we shall be able to trace this development as it can be seen along the banks of the river.

Geologically, the river's formation is unusual in that the St Lawrence, like the Great Lakes, flows from west to east, while other great river systems of North America flow from north to south.

Although the river itself is only 1,287 km (800 miles) long, modern engineering has made it possible for ships to sail along it to the Great Lakes. Altogether this great waterway, flowing into the heart of the North American continent, covers a route of more than 4,800 km (3,000 miles). Our journey will take us along a part of this route, from

Right *A lighthouse on Prince Edward Island in the gulf of the St Lawrence river*

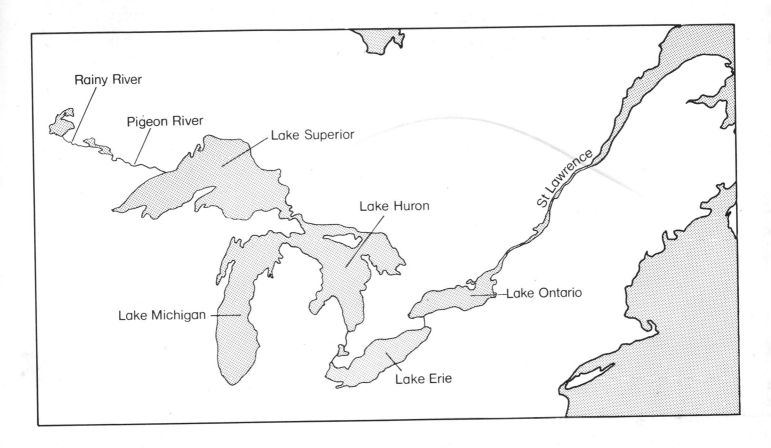

Above *A map of the whole river and lakes system from the Atlantic Ocean to the interior of Canada*

Left *This picture, taken from space, shows Lake Ontario (top), the city of Toronto, and the Niagara river leading into Lake Erie (bottom left)*

the Gulf of St Lawrence to Lake Ontario and Niagara Falls.

It was this waterway – the 'Lawrentian system' – that made it possible for the French, and later the British, to travel far into the interior of North America. This ability to travel so far inland had two important results. Firstly, it established a system of trade and communication which led the settlers in Canada to continue trading with Europe, rather than with the United States, for the St Lawrence

points like an arrow out across the Atlantic Ocean to the British ports. Secondly, the lakes and river system led to the early Canadian economy being based on a single major product: furs. The highly prized furs of beavers, foxes and musquash were

Above *The great St Lawrence is now tamed by man's engineering skills. This painting shows the first lock being built on the river in 1781*

Right *An early map of Canada.*

D. de Forbisher
Terres
Arctiques
D. de Hudson
D. de Dauis
OCEAN
SEPTEMTRIONAL
C. Faruuel
MER
CHRISTI
ANE
N. PAIS DE GALLES
Buttons Bay
Golfe de Hudson
TERRE DE LABRADOR et de CORTEREAL ou N. BRETAGNE
Baye Sauuage
Brest
Passage du Nort
Saguenay
Golfe de S. Laurens
I. de Terre Neuue
Kiristinous.
Nepiciriniens
CANADA
Tadousac
QVEBEC
Lac Superieur
LE N. FRANCE
Accadie
C. Breton
Le grand Banc.
I. de Sable
Lac des puants
MER DOVCE
Algonquins
Huron
Nation des Puants
Iroquois
Boston
N. ANGLETERRE
N. Plymout
Orange
PAIS-BAS ou Nle HOLANDE
Amsterdam
Christina
Lac du Chat
FLORIDE
VIRGINIE
Nle SVEDE
Mer de Canada
B. Chesapeak
MER DE NORT
CANADA

Above *A North American beaver. These animals provided the early settlers with valuable furs for export to Europe*

Left *Beavers build huge dams of logs and sticks, like this one, by felling trees. The dams raise the level of the water in the pond and enable the beavers to live safely in their home at the centre of the pond*

brought out from the interior of the continent to be sold in the markets of Europe.

The Indians, the original inhabitants of the country, became traders too. The Iroquois, or people of the Long House, lived to the south of the river, where they farmed. The Hurons, another

tribe, also led an agricultural life. Animosity between the tribes grew stronger when the 'white men' came. The Indian tribes fought each other to gain control of the best trapping lands so that they could have the best trading opportunities.

'White men', or Europeans, first came to the St Lawrence for certain in 1534, when Jacques Cartier, sailing for the king of France, entered the Bay of Chaleur, rounded the point of the Gaspé Peninsula, and visited Anticosti Island in the mouth of the river. Like all the early explorers in this area, he was, in fact, looking for a trade route to China.

Left *A drawing of Cartier and his men sailing up the newly-discovered St Lawrence*

Below *Jacques Cartier, the first European to explore the river*

The next year, when the ice had melted and navigation was again possible, Cartier sailed up the St Lawrence, naming the bay in which he moored his boat the 'Baye Saint Laurens', as it was the day of the feast of St Lawrence. This name was later given to the gulf and the river itself.

Cartier found the coasts of Labrador so barren that he called them 'the land God gave to Cain'. Later, he sailed up the river to a Huron Indian village called Hochelaga. Here he went ashore and climbed a great hill, which he called Mont Royal, the 'royal mountain'. This later became the site of Montreal. As the story goes, the Indians pointed on up the river and said 'Kanata'. Cartier thought they were telling him the name of the country; actually they were naming an Indian village. And that is how Canada received its name.

When the first explorers came to the St Lawrence they found it impassable in places, for there were wild and powerful rapids blocking the way to ships. Today, however, the St Lawrence Seaway – a great water route made up of the river, the lakes, and various linking canals – enables large ocean-going ships to sail right up the river to the Great Lakes and beyond. Man has also learned how to harness the river's force and turn it into electric power.

As we journey up the St Lawrence, we shall see some of the many facets of this great river: its strength, its importance in history, its wildlife, and its use as a transport system and source of power.

Right *Much of the St Lawrence is frozen in the winter months. This nineteenth-century drawing shows men cutting the ice*

From ocean to river

We are going to start our journey up the St Lawrence just as Cartier may have started his first expedition. We board our boat at Gaspé, which means 'the end of the world'. The Gaspé Peninsula is at the beginning of the Gulf of St Lawrence. Here there are limestone cliffs, shingly beaches, streams and coves. Small fishing boats cluster about the wharves, not

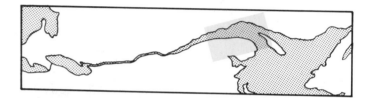

having changed much since the 1700s. The codfish from the fishing boats is still split, salted and dried on wooden racks along the beach, just as it was then.

On the other side of the peninsula is Cap-de-Rosiers, named after the wild roses that grow there. This is where the St Lawrence officially ends, flowing into the Gulf of St Lawrence. The coast here is very dangerous and until a short while ago a cannon was fired every hour in snow and fog to warn ships. If we had been sailing past the Cap-de-Rosiers in the 1800s, flags would have signalled our arrival to towns all along the river.

Percé Rock, a great spire 88m (288 ft) high, stands at the tip of the Gaspé Peninsula. It has been

Left *Percé Rock and village*

Right *A ship makes its way through the wintry landscape*

described as a giant stone horse standing in the gulf. In the seventeenth century there were, it is said, as many as four arches at the base of this massive sea sculpture. Today we can see only the one remaining arch. The Percé Rock got its name because the arches were made by the water piercing through the rock.

As we begin our journey we see that here the wildlife of the river and the gulf merge. Swallows are said to be the spirit of the great river, as they cluster around old, almost-deserted wharves during the summer months. Beginning in September, great white clouds of birds cover the sky. These are the greater snow geese, arriving from Greenland and the polar north where they have spent the summer. The snow geese spend autumn in the marshes along the river and then move south into the United States for the winter months.

Long ago, flocks of wild pigeons stopped along the St Lawrence on their migratory passage. They drew near the ground at sundown, with their wild cries filling the air, to fall to their feeding grounds. But this species, called the passenger pigeon, was easy to shoot. Once there was a population of millions; now they have been completely exterminated.

There is a great variety of wildlife in this stretch of the river, some belonging to the freshwater river, some belonging to the sea. Only about 64 km (40 miles) below Quebec City there are marine algae (sea plants) on one side of the bank and freshwater

Left *Snow geese and blue geese migrating along the river*

Above *Grebes on the frozen St Lawrence*

plants on the other. Because of this mixture of habitats, the eel is common in the St Lawrence. In fact, its journey west is only halted by the barrier of the Niagara Falls. Eels are nocturnal creatures and prefer bad weather to good. They plunge and dart in the dark waters and most people do not even notice that they are there. At one time a great deal of eel fishing was done during the months of September and October. Special traps, great cages of wood and wire, were placed in the shallow waters of the river.

One of the other common inhabitants of the St Lawrence is the sturgeon, a large fish – green with a white belly – that can grow to as much as 3m (10 ft) in length.

As we continue our journey upstream we sail through part of the province of Quebec. The river banks are still far apart and often thickly covered with trees.

25

French Canada and Quebec

The province of Quebec is unlike any other province in Canada. It was settled by the French in the 1600s and still maintains a French way of life. The people are French Canadians, who speak French and worship in Roman Catholic churches. Most of the French Canadians live on small farms along the St Lawrence river or in the two large cities, Montreal and Quebec.

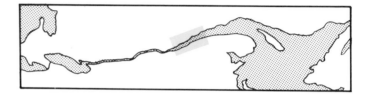

Right *An early French Canadian farmhouse*

Below *A ferryboat breaks through the ice at Quebec*

At this point we join a cruise-ship for a short while so that we might get a chance to see whales where the Saguenay river joins the St Lawrence. The shallow waters here provide excellent food for whales, mostly consisting of shrimp-like crustaceans called krill. Tours for whale sightings are quite common on this stretch of the river. It has been suggested that the whales may in fact be coming to see the people clustered about the boat railings!

Our ship sails out to where the river is so wide that only one shore is visible at a time. The trips begin early in the morning and even in August it is necessary to wrap up warmly. All the preparations are made worthwhile by the sight of these great mammals gliding through the water. The beluga, or white whale, was once so common in the river that it was named the 'St Lawrence whale'. Blue whales, minkes and finbacks are also seen here. Whalers once hunted whales to obtain their oil; today there is very little hunting allowed as many of the species are in danger of becoming extinct.

The St Lawrence is, of course, mainly used for transport, not for sight-seeing. A large lumber (timber) industry has grown up along the river and barges take the lumber from the forest downstream to the paper mills on the shore.

Returning to our journey up the river, we now

Left *Fine forestland in Quebec province*

Right *The Parc des Laurentides, north of Quebec, is an excellent place to learn to ski*

Above *The church of Saint Anne de Beaupré, famous for its faith-healing shrine*

pass through French Canadian territory, with numerous farms all along the banks. The original French farmers – called *habitants* – settled along these banks. They cleared the forest and laid out long narrow strips of farmland running down to the river. Many of these farmsteads still survive.

As we sail by we can still see the wooden French Canadian farmhouses, built with steeply sloping roofs so that snow will slip off them easily. The other buildings are placed close by for protection, but not so close as to create a fire hazard. Long ago we would have seen women baking bread, using outdoor ovens to cut down the risk of fire in the wooden farmhouse.

Even now the French Canadians have preserved many of their old songs, skills and handicrafts. In some of the old farmhouses you might still find someone using a spinning wheel, or a hand loom, or making a rug.

But a great deal of French Canadian life has now changed. As we move up the broad river we shall see television towers, busy roadways, and, along the south shore, the great Trans-Canada Highway. This road links Newfoundland to the west of Canada in a single ribbon of concrete and asphalt.

One stop before we reach Quebec is especially important to French Canadians: the Beaupré Coast, on the north shore of the St Lawrence. It is most famous for the faith-healing shrine of Saint Anne de Beaupré. Many French Canadians remain devoted Roman Catholics, and more than a million visit this shrine every year. Some come to pray; some are merely curious; others come looking for a miraculous cure. Here are said to be the bones of Saint Anne, which are believed to contain great healing powers.

It is not long before we reach the sheer cliffs of Quebec. The Indian name for Quebec means 'place where the water narrows'. At the beginning of our journey from the gulf the north and south banks of the St Lawrence were far apart. But now the river narrows, allowing us to view both banks as we sail further upstream.

Right *An old drawing of the fortress built on the high cliffs at Quebec city*

Samuel de Champlain, a French explorer, arrived here in 1608. Like Cartier half a century before, Champlain sailed down the St Lawrence from the gulf. Here, where the river was only 1.6 km (1 mile) wide, and where there were high cliffs from which to

Above *Children playing in a snowy Quebec street*

Right *Quebec harbour, with its modern docks and skyscrapers*

defend themselves from attack, Champlain and his men built a wooden fort — the original settlement of Quebec. By North American standards Quebec is ancient, for it is older than any other city north of Mexico.

Quebec City stands today much as it did several hundred years ago. Champlains's first buildings were

Left *A street in Quebec's old town*

Right *Château Frontenac, a nineteenth-century hotel, overlooks modern Quebec and the river*

Below *An old French Canadian house in the city*

sited between the river and the cliffs. Later the settlement spread to the top of Cape Diamond, 107 m (350 ft) above the river. The massive Château Frontenac, a nineteenth-century hotel built on Cape Diamond, is the only tall building to mar the seventeenth-century skyline.

We shall take a short ride in a *calèche* (a horse-drawn vehicle) to get a better view of the old part of the city. Quebec claims to be the only walled city in North America. Its fortifications are most impressive, as indeed they needed to be, for the city has been besieged six times. The last occasion was in 1759 when, at the Battle of Quebec, General Wolfe defeated the French and delivered Quebec, then the capital of French Canada, into the hands of the English.

The lower town, with its old stone houses and tile roofs, is still bustling with life. Houses, churches, and monuments are all huddled together along cobbled, narrow streets.

The other half of Quebec is modern, although still distinctly French. Much industry has grown up here, and the hydro-electric power provided by the St Lawrence is used in the paper, leather and engineering industries. At one time Quebec was as far upriver as large ships could go, but now the river has been deepened. Today the largest ships can call at Quebec and then pass on upriver to Montreal.

Left *The St Lawrence Seaway at Quebec*
Right *Cape Diamond and Château Frontenac*

Three Rivers

We must now sail on towards Three Rivers. In the winter the St Anne river, on our right, is frozen solid. From December to February each year a community of fishermen springs up on this frozen river. They live on the frozen surface and fish for tommycod through holes in the ice. They can fish only so long as the ice is thick enough to hold the weight of their temporary 'town'.

Three Rivers (or Trois Rivières) is the second oldest city in Canada, founded in 1634. The city was built up where the St Lawrence and St Maurice

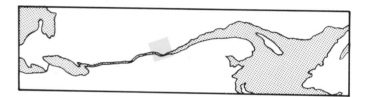

rivers join. It is here that the St Lawrence first becomes a tidal river on its way to the gulf. (A tidal river is one in which the tides of the sea can be felt, as the water level rises and falls.)

The city of Three Rivers is built up on a series of terraces overlooking the river. It possesses more seventeenth and eighteenth-century buildings than any other place in Canada or the United States. Many of these old buildings have escaped destruction by developers because Montreal has taken over as the centre of activity. In the nineteenth century many paper mills were built here, making paper from logs that were floated down from the forests. Paper is still a major industry in Three Rivers.

Left *Fishing through holes in the ice of a frozen river*

Right *Canada's rivers provide excellent transport for its timber industry. These logs are being floated down the Ottawa river on their way to the St Lawrence*

Above *A bright patch of fireweed*

Now that the river is completely freshwater, the wildlife changes. Muskellunge, a large freshwater fish, is found here. Common gallinules (water hens), and long-billed and short-billed wrens are all found along the banks of the wide Lake St Peter (Lac Saint Pierre), in the section of the St Lawrence just below Three Rivers. Numerous wild flowers, such as asters, fireweed (rose-bay willowherb) and violets are common along the banks.

Left *A child samples a Canadian delicacy – maple syrup – which is collected from maple trees in the spring*

Right *An aerial view of the town of Three Rivers*

41

Montreal

Montreal, the largest city in Canada, is the next stop on our journey. It is built on a 50 km (31 miles) long island in the St Lawrence. The original settlement, begun in 1642, survived fifty years of Indian attacks and grew into the capital of the fur trade in the 1700s. Now it is the second-largest French-speaking city in the world, with a population of nearly three million. It is also Canada's largest manufacturing city and an important business centre. Even though much of

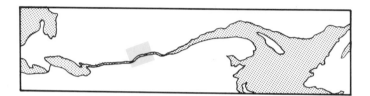

Right *Montreal today, with its high-rise office blocks*
Below *Montreal in the nineteenth century*

Above *Although it is so far from the sea, Montreal is one of the world's greatest inland seaports*

Left *A street and church in old Montreal*

Montreal is modern, with skyscrapers silhouetted against the sky, old and new buildings often stand side by side.

Not only has a modern city sprung up where frontier settlers once lived, but now beneath the pavement there is also an underground city. Here there is a maze of shops, theatres, restaurants and offices, connected by passageways and the underground railway — the Metro. In the middle of winter, when the temperature is far below zero and the St Lawrence is covered in ice, the people of Montreal have their modern underground community to provide them with everything they need.

Montreal also brings together the French and

English-speaking cultures of Canada. It is within French Canada but is inhabited by peoples of many cultural backgrounds. Many Europeans have emigrated to Montreal, where they mingle with the older French and English communities.

As well as being a business and industrial centre, Montreal has outstanding academic facilities, too, with major universities and research centres. In fact, Montreal is bustling with anything that strikes the imagination and, as in most large international cities, its nightlife continues until the early hours. It has now taken over from Quebec and Three Rivers as the most important city of the St Lawrence.

During the American Revolution in 1776, Benjamin Franklin journeyed to Montreal to ask the French to join the American War of Independence. The French refused to do so, for they preferred to remain loyal to the British. They were satisfied with living under the British because they were allowed to keep their own way of life. It is possible that, if they had joined the American Revolution, the British Canadian provinces might well have become American too.

For Canada, the most important result of the American Revolution was the introduction of a new group of people into the country. Thousands of former British subjects who had opposed the revolution were still living in the American colonies. They were known as Loyalists. These people were taken into Canada by the British and settled in Nova

Left *Montreal and the St Lawrence, seen from the top of one of the city's many modern buildings*

Above *The St Lawrence and the port of Montreal at sunset*

Scotia, along the St Lawrence just below Montreal, and on the Niagara frontier.

The Loyalists came in two major waves, during the American Revolution and a few years after it ended in 1783, when the new United States had confiscated their lands. They became especially strong in their sense of Canadian national identity, for they had fled from the revolution so that they might remain loyal to their British king. All along the southern bank of the St Lawrence, stretching out toward the American border, the Loyalists took up new land in what became known as the Eastern Townships.

Through the Seaway

Although the St Lawrence is now part of one of the world's greatest inland trade routes – stretching from the Atlantic to the head of Lake Superior – it was not formed that way by nature. As the early explorers found, stretches of dangerous rapids, frozen water in the winter, and variations in water level between one lake and another all stood in their way. These hazards have now been overcome by the use of ice-breaking ships (at least as far upriver as Montreal) and the completion of vast engineering

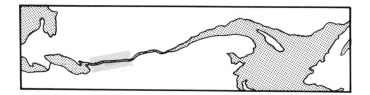

Right *An oil tanker makes it way through the Seaway*

Below *This diagram shows a cross-section through the whole river and lakes system. The many changes in level have now been overcome by the building of great locks and canals*

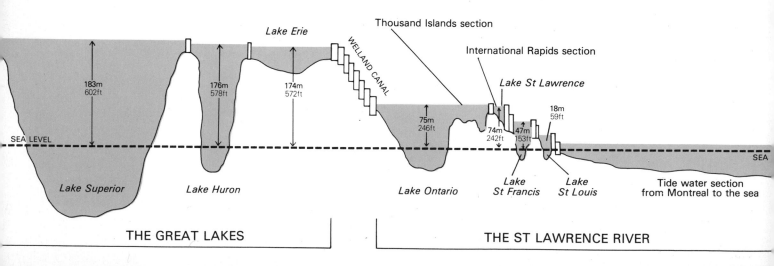

Lake Erie

Thousand Islands section

International Rapids section

Lake St Lawrence

WELLAND CANAL

183m 602ft

176m 578ft

174m 572ft

75m 246ft

74m 242ft

47m 153ft

18m 59ft

SEA LEVEL

SEA

Lake Superior

Lake Huron

Lake Ontario

Lake St Francis

Lake St Louis

Tide water section from Montreal to the sea

THE GREAT LAKES

THE ST LAWRENCE RIVER

works. There are canals to bypass the rapids and locks to lift ships from one level to another.

As we leave Montreal we sail into the St Lawrence Seaway, which is part of this trade route. The most difficult part of the river to control was this section between Montreal and Kingston, where there were many rapids. Firstly, the engineers built a dam across the river, forming a new lake (Lake St Lawrence) which drowned out some of the rapids. Many villages had to be moved out of the way of the rising waters of the new lake. Canals, with lift locks that raise the ships to the next level, were constructed. Below the dam a huge hydro-electric power station was built, belonging to Canada and the United States, and using the river's power to make electricity for both countries.

The problems involved in harnessing the river were enormous. During the winter, for example, engineers had to find ways to stop the cement freezing before it had time to set. However, in 1959 this joint Canadian-U.S. project was completed. Queen Elizabeth II sailed from the Gulf of St Lawrence to Montreal in the royal yacht and, together with President Eisenhower of the United States, opened the St Lawrence Seaway. Now thousands of ships pass through the Seaway each year, many of them carrying grain or iron ore.

The St Lawrence and the Great Lakes waterway, taken together, form the longest inland navigation system in North America. Even ocean-going ships can reach as far as about 4,000 km (2,500 miles) inland, using the deep canals and giant locks.

Three hundred years ago, however, it was not only the rapids that made this section of the river dangerous. It was here, at the Long Sault (an island in the St Lawrence) that one of the most fearsome battles was fought between the Iroquois and Huron Indians and the French. In 1660 a small group of inexperienced French trappers set off in search of furs. Stranded on floating ice, they were rescued by

Left *Canals and locks on the Seaway near Iroquois*

Right *A cargo ship entering one of the Seaway's many locks*

Hurons and Algonquins, who then journeyed with them to Long Sault. They had been there only a short time when four Iroquois, who were enemies of the French, arrived. The French ambushed them, but one Iroquois escaped and brought back a force of 200 Iroquois warriors. Both sides prepared to defend themselves and the Iroquois attacked vigorously. Soon, 500 more warriors joined the battle. All but two of the Hurons and Algonquins deserted the French and, on the eighth day, the Indians broke into the French fort and massacred all the remaining French people.

Further upriver, between Brockville (one of the first Loyalist settlements in Upper Canada) and Gananoque (now a Canadian resort town) we reach the Thousand Islands. These famous islands provide summer homes and marinas for hundreds of people. Eighteen of the islands have been declared a National Park. Some have been given poetic names, such as Camelot, Mermaid and Endymion.

The Indians called the islands the 'Garden of the Great Spirit'. The legend is that the Great Spirit created a garden paradise to help bring peace to the tribes that were constantly at war with one another. Yet, even with this paradise, the Indians still fought, so the Great Spirit gathered his paradise into a blanket and flew towards his home in the heavens. On his journey the blanket tore and paradise crashed

Left *This section of road and railway rises to allow ships to pass underneath.*

Right *A view along a section of the Seaway*

into the river, breaking into thousands of pieces.

The scientific explanation for these islands is very different. According to this explanation, the islands are the tops of low hills (the worn-down remains of ancient mountains) which thrust above the level of the river.

The Thousand Islands area, with its beauty and peace, is a splendid place for a holiday. There is a rich variety of wildlife to study, for there are 65 bird

Above *50 million tons of cargo, carried in ships from all over the world, pass through the Seaway each year*

Right *A complete contrast — the small pleasure boats of the Thousand Islands holiday area*

species in the islands, including red-breasted mergansers. Trees with names like blackoak, mayapple, shaggymane and deer berry can be found growing here.

Journey to Niagara

When we reach Kingston we are almost on the waters of Lake Ontario, where the St Lawrence begins. Kingston, once an Indian village, then a French fortress and later a British citadel, was also a Canadian capital. In 1673 Governor Frontenac built a wooden stockade here. La Salle, the French explorer, replaced it with stone and named it Fort

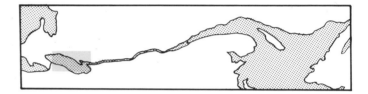

Frontenac. In 1784 it was retaken by the British and given the name Kingston, after King George III of England. Today Kingston is an important military and naval base, and the site of the Royal Military College. One of the most important figures in the history of Canada came from Kingston. This was Sir John A. Macdonald, the 'Father of Canada'. He began his career as a lawyer in Kingston, but his real interest was in politics.

It was Macdonald who helped to create a united and independent Canada. The move toward union between the peoples of Canada had begun in the

Left *The fort at Kingston*

Right *The courthouse in Kingston, built in classical style*

Above *The maple leaf symbol of Canada on the national flag*

Brunswick, Quebec and Ontario agreed to unite.

At first the St Lawrence river dominated the politics of the new nation. The capital alternated between Montreal and Toronto. This was an unsatisfactory arrangement, however, and the Canadians asked Britain's Queen Victoria for her advice as to a site for their national capital. She chose neither of the old colonial sites. Instead, she chose a tiny village well up a tributary of the St Lawrence, on the banks of the Ottawa river. There grew up the city of Ottawa, the capital of present-day Canada.

Right *The fine buildings of the Canadian parliament in Ottawa*

Below *Changing the guard outside the parliament buildings in Ottawa, the capital city of Canada*

1840s. By the 1860s, when the United States was in the midst of a great civil war, Canadians realized that they must unite or they might well be annexed by the United States at the end of the war. It was Macdonald, working with the French Canadian leader Georges Etienne Cartier and other political figures, who brought this about. The Canadian leaders negotiated with each other to form a confederation. The new country – the Confederation of the Dominion of Canada – came into being on July 1st 1867, when Nova Scotia, New

Now we are almost at the end of our journey. The St Lawrence officially begins at the north-eastern end of Lake Ontario. However, this is not its 'source' in the usual sense, for much of the water which runs from here to the Atlantic has its origin in the Great Lakes and the vast drainage area of more than 1,760,000 sq km (680,000 sq miles). We shall, therefore, travel just a little further into the Great Lakes, with which the St Lawrence system is linked.

On Lake Ontario is the city of Toronto, the capital of the province of Ontario. This province is very different from that of Quebec. From the outset Ontario was settled by English-speaking people and its system of law is based on English laws rather than French.

Toronto was first established as York in 1793, largely by Loyalists who had left America. It was built as a capital and was thought to be safe from attack. However, the Americans captured it during their war with Britain in 1812-15, and much of the city had to be rebuilt in 1834.

Toronto is the largest city of English-speaking Canada. One of the best-planned cities in the world, Toronto has managed to keep part of its former wilderness, for the city is built along a series of largely unspoiled ravines, some with rivers running through them. Signs in the parks encourage people to 'Please Walk on the Grass'. Yet here live over two million people in the second-largest city in Canada.

When the early settlers arrived here, the areas around Lake Ontario and Lake Erie were inhabited by the *coureurs de bois,* or 'runners of the forest'. These were unlicensed French fur traders who either lived with Indian tribes or who stayed away for two to three years in search of furs. Many *coureurs de bois* married Indian girls.

With their wives, these traders started fur-trading posts of their own, developing a new culture which was a mixture of French and Indian. The children were brought up as Roman Catholics. As these people moved further west, they became known as the *Métis.* By the late nineteenth century they were an important factor in the settlement of Manitoba and Saskatchewan.

Niagara Falls is where we shall end our travels, though we could follow the waters through the Great Lakes into the heart of the North American continent. Many thousands of years ago, old lakes were being reborn and new ones created as the Ice Age came to an end. One such lake was Lake Erie. As thawing continued, Lake Erie found a new outlet for its rising water through the Niagara river into Lake Ontario. To do this the water was forced to plunge some 60m (197 ft) over a high escarpment — thus creating Niagara Falls.

To get a true sense of the strength of these thundering waters, let us take an aerocar suspended above the falls. From there we can see the full power of the falls, which were first sighted in 1679 by Jean-Louis Hennepin, a Belgian missionary and explorer.

Right *Toronto, the largest city of English-speaking Canada, seen from Lake Ontario*

The waters of Lake Erie feed the never-ending torrent of water. As early as 1829 work began to build a series of canals which would enable ships to pass the falls and reach the level of Lake Erie. Since then the canals have been rebuilt several times to

Above *Containers and a container ship in Toronto harbour*

Right *The old trails of the Indians and* coureurs de bois, *now widened for the modern hiker, still survive along the banks of the upper St Lawrence*

make room for more and more traffic, and larger ships. The Welland canal, with its eight locks, is now a very important part of the Seaway, enabling ships from the Great Lakes to reach the St Lawrence river and ships from the river to reach the Great Lakes.

When engineers discovered how to turn water-power into electricity, using hydro-electric schemes, a power-house was built beside Niagara Falls and some of its water was diverted to pass through turbines. These turbines drive the electric generators.

This turning of the water's power into electricity is a further example of the way in which man has been able to alter and use natural resources for his own purposes. When the first explorers came to Canada, the St Lawrence was the doorway through which they penetrated the interior of the continent. Today, with man's intervention, the river is an international routeway leading out into the rest of the world.

At one point, for about 161 km (100 miles), the St Lawrence forms the boundary between Canada and the United States. There the two governments have placed a stone with an inscription which summarizes the history of both nations:

'This stone bears witness to the common purpose of two nations whose frontiers are the frontiers of friendship, whose ways are the ways of freedom, and whose works are the works of peace.'

Left *This paddle steamer in Toronto harbour enables tourists to travel in the grand old style*

Right *The Niagara Falls span the Canadian-American border. This is a view of the American side of the falls and Niagara town from the observation tower on the Canadian side*

Further reading

Brookes, Ivan S. *The Lower St Lawrence* (Freshwater, 1974)

Creighton, Donald *The Story of Canada* (Faber, 1971; Houghton Mifflin, 1960)

Ferguson, Linda *Canada* (Scribner, 1979)

Gough, Barry M. (ed.) *Canada* (Prentice-Hall, 1975)

Harris, Jeannette *Canada* (Silver Burdett Co., 1976)

Hills, Theo L. & Sarah Jane *Canada* (Fideler, 1979)

Judson, Clara Ingram *The St Lawrence Seaway* (Wheaton, 1966)

Toye, William *Cartier Discovers the St Lawrence* (Oxford University Press, 1971)

Watson, Jane Werner *Giant of the North* (Garrard, 1968)

White, Anne T. *The St Lawrence Seaway* (Frederick Muller, 1962; Garrard, 1961)

Films: the National Film Board of Canada is well known for its films. Some of these films can be borrowed from the National Film Board of Canada, 16th Floor, 1251 Avenue of the Americas, New York, N.Y. 10020, or from the Canadian High Commission, Canada House, Trafalgar Square, London. For information, write to the Embassy of Canada, Massachusetts Avenue, Washington D.C. To pursue a particular subject, look at H. C. Campbell's little book *How to Find Out About Canada* (Pergamon Press, Oxford, 1967).

Glossary

Algae Family of simple plants (including seaweed), almost all of which live in water.

Confederation Union of separate political states into one nation.

Dam Man-made barrier across a river, forming a lake behind it.

Dominion A self-governing country of the former British Empire.

Gallinule Waterbird resembling a small hen; also called the marsh hen or water hen.

Geology Study of the formation and structure of the crust of the earth.

Gulf Indentation in a coastline.

Habitant Early French-speaking settler in Canada.

Hydro-electric power Electric power produced by using the force of water to drive turbines.

Lock Section of a river or canal closed off by gates so that the water level can be altered to move ships to higher or lower levels.

Logging Cutting down trees to produce timber.

Loyalist English-speaking settler, loyal to Britain, who left America after the Civil War and moved to Canada.

Métis Partially French, partially Indian inhabitants of the Canadian West.

Muskellunge Large fish; the North American pike.

Peninsula Piece of land jutting out into the water.

Province Separate political unit belonging to an empire or a state.

Quebecois Resident of Quebec.

Rapids Steep descent in a river bed with a swift and often dangerous current.

Stockade Wooden fence built to protect the people behind it from attack

Tommycod Fish resembling cod but much smaller.

Waterway A water route, either natural or a combination of natural lakes and rivers linked by canals.

Facts and figures

Length of the St Lawrence: 1,287 km (800 miles).

Great Lakes: surface area approximately 246,000 sq km (95,000 sq miles) — slightly larger than Great Britain.

St Lawrence Seaway: total length from Duluth (on Lake Superior) to the Atlantic: 3,769 km (2,342 miles).

Locks: 16 locks overcome a drop of 177m (580 ft) from the head of Lake Superior to Montreal.

Cargo tonnage: 50 million tons annually. The Seaway is open for shipping during eight months of the year. During the winter months ice makes navigation impossible. Various schemes have been suggested to overcome this problem but all have, so far, proved too costly to put into operation.

Quebec province: area nearly three times the size of France. Population: 6½ million.

Ontario province: area twice the size of Spain. Population: 8½ million.

Canada: area 9,975,185 sq km (3,851,809 sq miles) — the second-largest country in the world. Population: 23 million.

Languages: 13 million Canadians use English as their mother tongue; 6 million use French; 4 million use other languages, including 200,000 Red Indian and Inuit (Eskimo) -speaking Canadians.

ACKNOWLEDGEMENTS

Aerofilms Library: 50; Aquila: 16 (Eric Soothill), 17 (Steve Downer), 24 (Edgar T. Jones), 25 (Edgar T. Jones), 41 top (Edgar T. Jones); J. Allan Cash: *frontispiece,* 11, 35, 36, 39, 43, 49, 51, 52, 58 bottom right, 61, 64, 65; NASA: 12; National Film Board of Canada: 58 top left; John Topham Picture Library: 20-1, 27, 28, 29 (Roland Weber), 31, 42, 46 (Pierre le Bihan), 47 (Roland Weber), 57. Photographs on pages .23, 26, 32, 32-3, 34, 37, 38, 44, 53, 54, 55, 59, 62 and 63 courtesy of the authors. Drawings on pages 15 and 18-19 from the Wayland Picture Library. The publishers wish to thank the Canadian High Commission and the Public Archives of Canada for the use of the pictures on pages 14, 19 bottom right, 22, 30, 40, 41 bottom right, and 56; the Montreal Municipal Tourist Board for the use of the photograph on page 45. Artwork by Alan Gunston.

Index